The Dancing Men Cypher

A fun secret code for kids of all ages

By R-Jay Wilde
2010

ISBN-13: 9798332107443

To Avery Grace Wilde, future super spy, who reintroduced me to the Dancing Men Cypher and to Sir Author Connon Doyle the genius who invented it.

Introduction: Why This Book

I wrote this book for my kids. Apart from my wife, they are my greatest inspiration. This book Introduces the dancing men cypher: what it is, where it came from, and most fun of all how to use it.

That is the short answer and of course, there is a longer answer to why I wrote this book. Since there is space here to share and you seem interested (you are still reading this), I will share the long story.

Once upon a time I harbored ambitions of going into the military. Really my goal was to go to college and the military offered one of the surest routes to paying for an advanced degree. Neither I nor my parents had saved any money for my future education and even in my younger years college was expensive. With some luck and hard work, two branches of the military awarded me scholarships and I found myself in one of my most interesting university classes, Military Science. While many useful bits of information came from this class, the most relevant here has to do with information and communication.

In the military you often have a large group of people working together toward a common goal, but most of those people are performing different tasks and missions. It is like a great dance; people need the right information at the right time to do their part of the job correctly. While you need information about your own people, you also need information about who or what you are fighting. The more information you have about the "enemy," the greater your chance of understanding them. Understanding you enemy is what helps you ether defeat them or turn them into an ally.

In the Art of War, Sun Tzu says, "If you know the enemy and know yourself, you need not fear the result of a hundred battles. If you know yourself but not the enemy, for every victory gained you will also suffer a defeat. If you know neither the enemy nor yourself, you will succumb in every battle." (Tzu, 2010)

Information is an advantage. If you have more information about your opponent than they have about you, then you increase your likelihood of winning. This is why militaries and corporations spend so much effort protecting what they consider to be valuable information. Now this is where codes and cyphers come into play and what the heck this has to do with my kids.

There is a popular book called Code Talker, by Joseph Bruchac, (Bruchac, 2006). It is a novel based on the vital work that Navajo Marines did during World War II. It comes back to this idea of protecting information. In World War II both sides of the conflict spent significant effort to protect their plans from each other. They had all kinds of secret codes, and even started using special coding machines to both create secret and decipher secret messages. Someone in the US had the brilliant idea of using Navajo solders to create a nearly unbreakable code. They used Navajo has the bases of creating words and phrases to communicate military plans among the Allied forces. Even when the Axis powers could overhear the coded messages, they could not understand it or even come close before the information was no longer of value. It gave the US a huge advantage. Since we won that war, one could argue that the Navao Code Talkers played a significant role in that victory.

My son, Jack, read Code Talkers and loved it. He kept wanting to talk about it. My youngest, Avery, hearing about code talkers from her brother, brought it up in one of her classes. This sparked some conversation in her class, which led to them doing some research and studying various codes. So now, we had two kids in the family talking about codes and cyphers. Before you knew it, this is what we were talking about at the dinner table. It included morse code, pig Latin, Turing's Enigma Breaker, modern encryption key algorithms, and many more. The world of codes and cyphers is vast and interesting. It is a bit of a rabbit hole if you chase after it. I would argue that is a fun rabbit whole where much is to be learned and glorious madness to be found.

Of all the codes we talked about, the one that fascinated me the most was the dancing men cypher. Avery showed me this one. Love at first site might be a little strong, but the idea of using little figures to communicate captured my imagination. Since that fateful spring of Wilde code exploration, the dancing men cypher has become an ever-growing part of my life.

One thing important to mention. This book is not meant to give anything close to a comprehensive understanding or knowledge of the fascinating world of Cryptography. It really is just an introduction to one simple and fun cypher. If you want to learn more about codes and cyphers, a quick search on the internet will show you the extensive list of resources out there.

With that said, I will still give you a very brief and simplified foundation of cyphers and codes.

A Very Brief History of Cyphers

What are codes and what are cyphers

Most people use the words code and cypher interchangeably. This gives the appearance that they mean the same thing. However, there is a subtle difference in their meaning. I did not know this before researching this book and only just discovered this important distinction.

Cyphers are a one-to-one replacement of written symbols. A common cypher is to replace letters with numbers. When you write the secret message it is just a string of numbers that must be turned into letters to reveal the words. Because of this one-to-one replacement, cyphers by themselves are generally pretty easy to solve.

Codes are more like a type of shorthand where you have words or short phrases that stand for something else. This is shown well in the movie Phenomena starring

John Travolta. The main character and his best friend are listening to the ham radio when they come across a channel used by the government. The main character realizes they are using Morse code (a cypher that replaces letters and numbers with dits and dahs). When they translates the Morse code they find that the government is talking about planting flowers in a garden. Eventually the main character figures out that the messages are a code for military commands. The garden stood for their area of operation and the various flowers and gardening activities represented military actions.

It is common to combine one or more cyphers with one or more codes. This is an effort to increase the complexity and therefor reduce the chance of someone figuring out the underlying message.

When doing research for this book, I came across an interesting piece of information about where they think the word Cypher comes from. In the middle ages in Europe, they used the Roman numeral system. In this system of numbers, there is no zero. This made the whole concept of zero difficult for Europeans to understand. The idea of zero came to Europe from the Arabic numeral system. The Arabic word for zero was "Sifr." In Latin, this word became "cifra." In French it became "cifre." Eventually in English it became "cipher." The theory is that because the concept of zero or cipher was so difficult to understand, that word became associated with anything that was difficult to understand, including coded messages (Ali-Karamali, 2008).

The Caesar Cypher

I love to read. Occasionally, in my literary journeys, I come across mentions of different codes and cyphers. Three have stayed with me over the years and are important for this book and represent some of the history of cyphers.

Earlier this year, I began a Louis Penny binge. Penny writes murder mystery books with exceptional character development. I often read them more to find out what is going on with the characters then to find out who killed who. It is like, "oh another person died, but really, I want to know when Ruth's duck is coming back." In the fifth book, The Brutal Telling, there appears to be several words carved into wood that are complete nonsense. As the story develops, the characters guess that it could be a cypher, more specifically a Caesar Cypher (Penny & Cosham, 2016).

Used by Julious Caesar, the Caesar Cypher is one of the earliest known. It is a substitution cypher where you replace one letter for a different letter. It requires the use of a key word or phrase to know how to displace the letters. A straightforward way to use this is to simply put the letters of the alphabet in alphabetical order. Then pick a word like my last name, Wilde. Wilde has five letters, so you shift the letters of the alphabet by five spaces. So A becomes E and B becomes F and so on through the alphabet until you get to U which becomes

Z. Then you start replacing the letters with those first five at the beginning, so V becomes A.

Below is a chart that shows the relationship.

Plain	A	B	C	D	E	F	G	H	I	J	K	L	M	N	O	P	Q	R	S	T	U	V	W	X	Y	Z
Cypher	V	W	X	Y	Z	A	B	C	D	E	F	G	H	I	J	K	L	M	N	O	P	Q	R	S	T	U

With this cypher the phrase "I love to read books" becomes "D gjqz oj mzvy wjjfn." Most people can solve this one in a short amount of time through trial and error. There are only 26 possible solutions. This cypher is fun to use, especially when combined with other cyphers or codes. If you want to learn more about the Caesar Cypher, there is a good article on Wikipedia that provides a more detailed explanation and lots of references in the bibliography.

Book Cypher

Several years ago I started reading The Change series by S.M. Sterling. In his book, The Protector's War, the characters discover several messages written in a numeric code that none of them can figure out. They eventually find a guy who is good at math to see what he can do with the code. He does not solve it but based on the patterns in the numbers theorizes that it is a book cypher or code (Stirling, 2006).

This is how it works. You write your message. Then you find a book that is known to both the sender and the receiver. The person writing the message takes each word of the message, finds that word in the book, and replaces the word with a series of numbers representing the page, line, and word.

Using the 1994 Haughton Mifflin publication of The Fellowship of the Rings by J.R.R. Tolkien, we could code "Went to the valley" to now be

67|41|10 295|21|15 260|25|5 135|27|13.

If you know which book to use, then this is an easy code to crack, though a bit time consuming. If you do not know the book to use, then it is next to impossible to solve.

Sir Arther Conan Doyle

Sir Arther Conan Doyle created Sherlock Holmes. He was a gifted writer and brilliant thinker. He is also why we even have the dancing men cypher. In his story The Adventure of the Dancing Men, the story begins with Holmes receiving a paper with a series of figures that appear to be dancing. Eventually Holmes figures out that the dancing figures are a substitution cypher and that the messages are quite threatening (Doyle, 1859-1930)

The whole story is a great commentary on how to crack an unknown code. It boils down to this, there are certain letters that appear more often than others and in regularly occurring patterns. By deduction you can begin to recognize some of the vowels and common consonants. Once you get a few letters, the others start to come together quickly. This approach works for most substitution cyphers. If you want to know more about the dancing men cypher there are several websites about it, including some that will translate regular text into dancing men text for you. At the very least, I recommend reading the Sherlock Holmes story. In fact, I included a copy of that story in this book.

My Use of the Dancing Men Cypher

I first read The Adventure of the Dancing Men many years ago. In fact I read every Sherlock Holmes story that Doyle ever wrote. Despite this, I had forgotten about the dancing men cypher until Avery reminded me.

My kids have always seemed to like games, puzzles, and adventure. They constantly surprise me with their willingness to try new things. Most people would agree that 2020 was a rough year. Covid and the associated restrictions and needed changes in behavior shook up how we perceive each other and the world. Our family did well. In many ways it was a time of great growth for us all. It did require me as a parent to step up my game a little bit. We have always been a creative bunch. Both my wife and I are artists and writers and so are my kids, but The restrictions of 2020 and 2021 forced us to dig deep and try many new things. A pirate treasure hunt complete with Goonies inspired map replaced trick or treating. A 35-foot zip line found itself in our smallish backyard (the sloping unevenness that makes mowing a bear, served well for the zip line). One of my favorite results was Easter of 2021, when we did a multilayer puzzle that included the dancing men cypher. This was my first time using the dancing men cypher and I include a copy of the puzzle later in this book.

The Dancing Men Cypher

What follows in this next section is the dancing men cypher. The original story reveals only part of the alphabet, but going online you can find the missing letters as well as numbers. In figuring out how best to share the dancing men cypher, I decided what I really needed was a font. So I created my own dancing men font. In doing that, I learned that for a full font there are 94 characters. 52 are the upper and lower case letters, 10 are the numbers 0-9, the rest are special characters like commas, periods, colons, etc.

For my font, I did not create all 94 characters the first time around. But what I did do is create the characters associated with the numbers on the keyboard. This is what I am giving you in the pages that follow. Eventually I will create the full-size font.

A a

B b

C c

D d

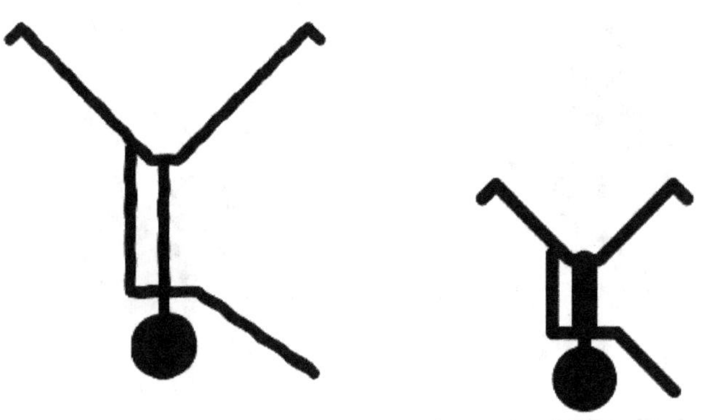

E e

F f

G g

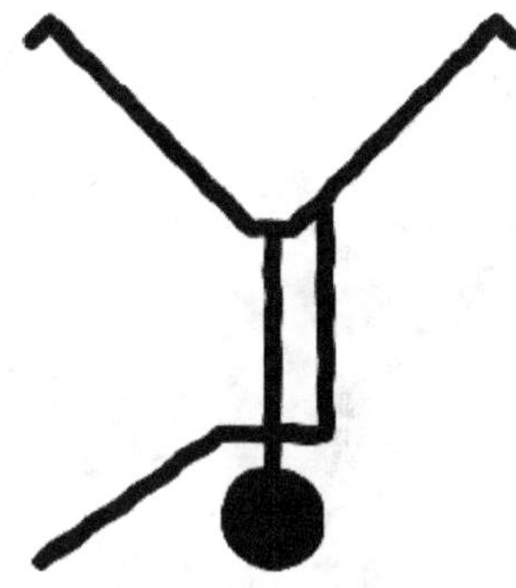

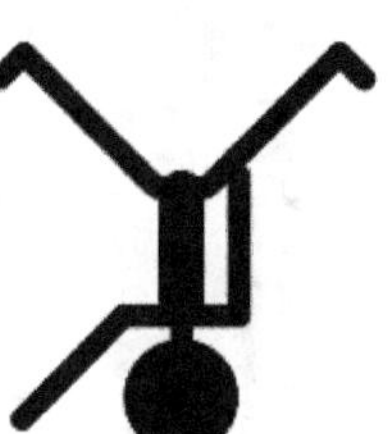

H h

J j

K k

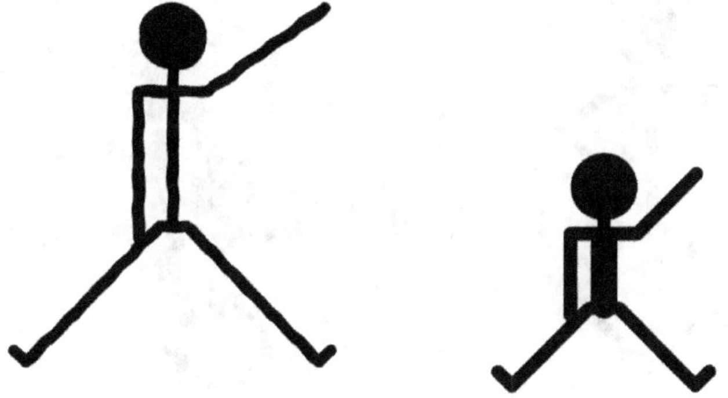

L l

M m

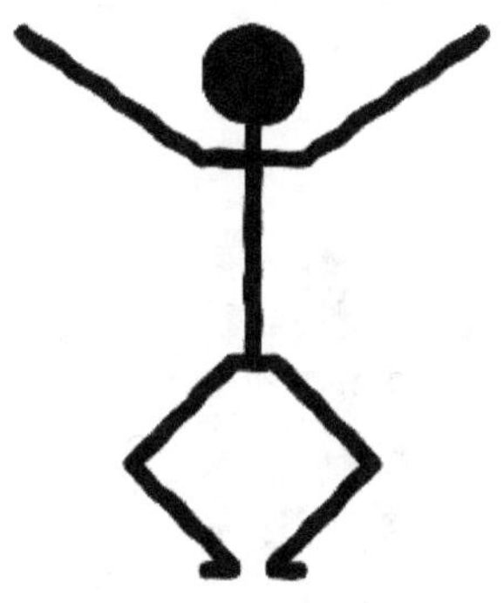 

N n

O o

P p

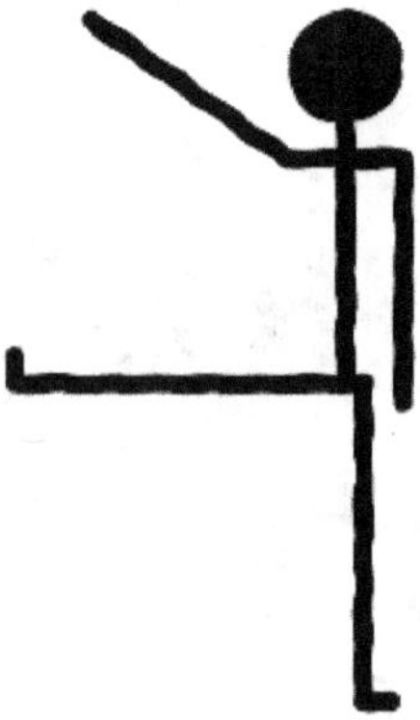

Q q

R r

S s

T t

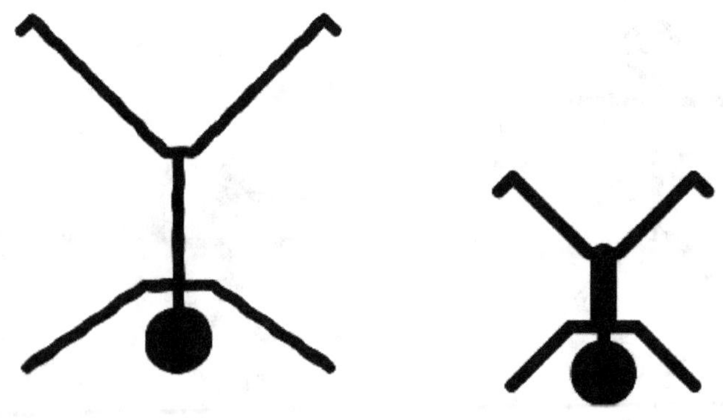

U u

V v

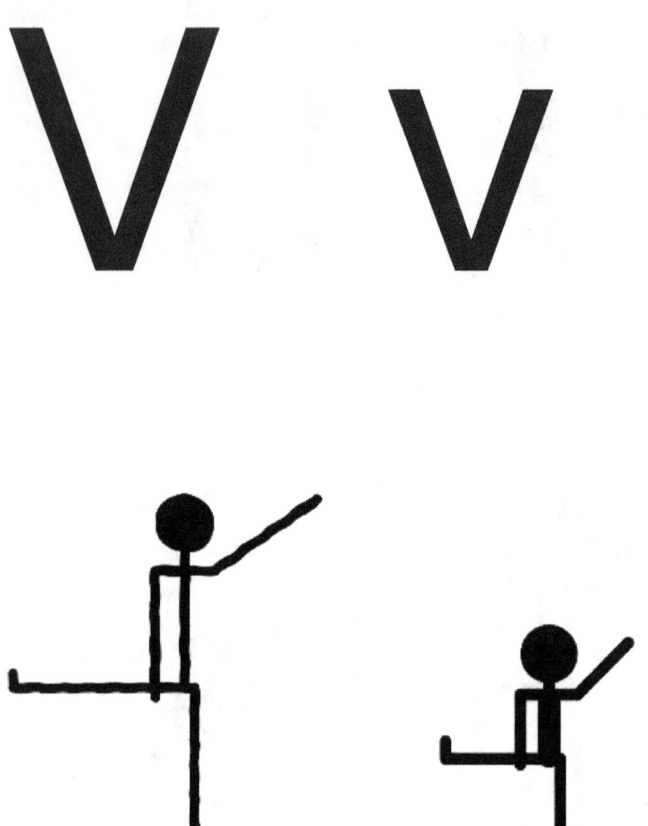

W w

X x

Y y

Z z

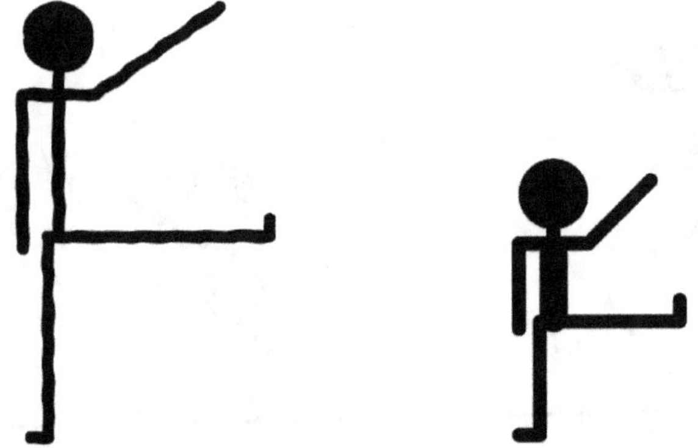

! ^

@ &

*

$ (

%)

Using the Dancing Men Cypher

Here is your chance to practice translating the cypher.
Hopefully there will be quotes you recognize.

Movie Quotes

Quote 1

Quote 2

Quote 3

Quote 4

Quote 5

Quote 6

Quote 7

Quote 8

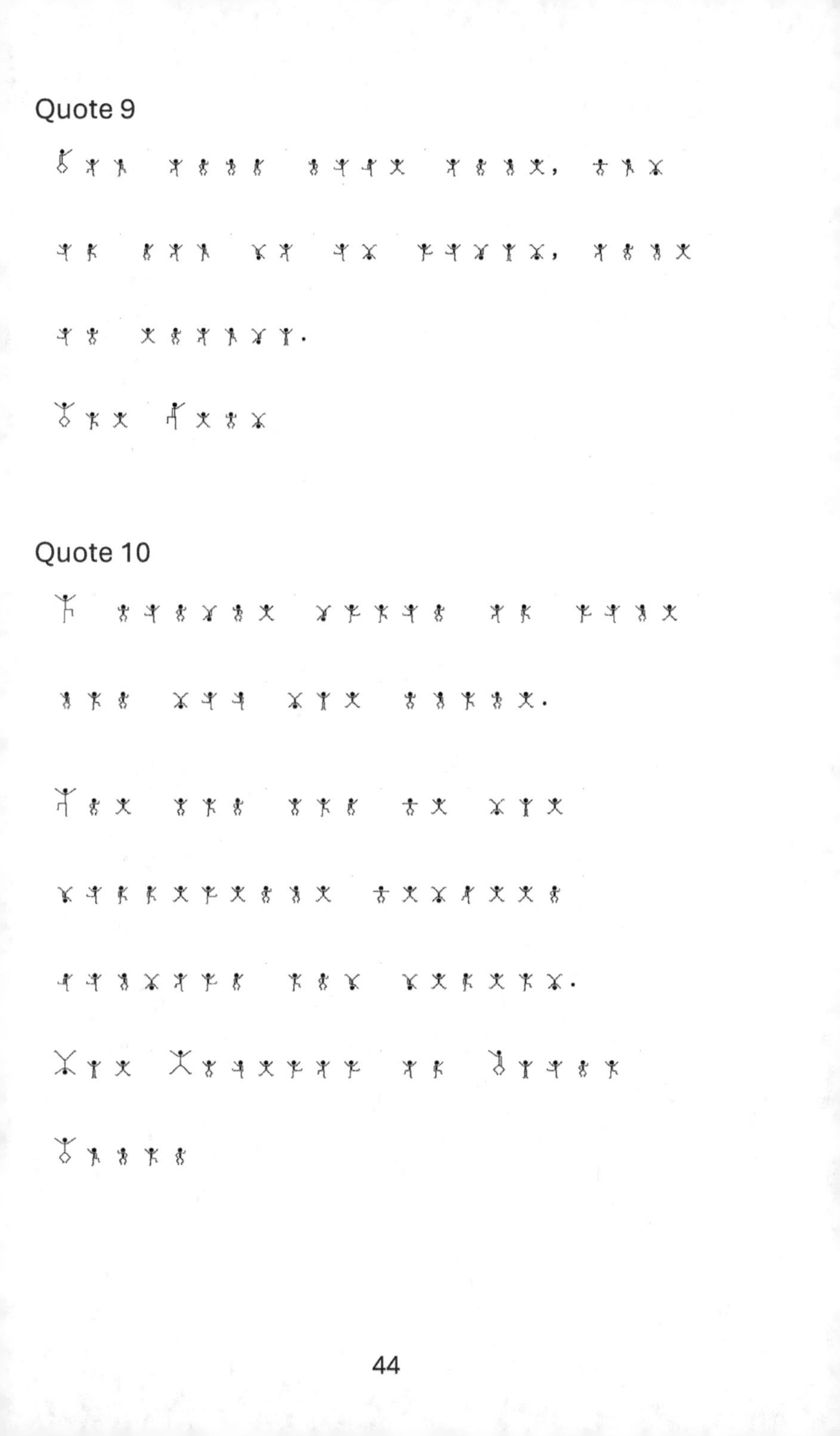

Quote 9

Quote 10

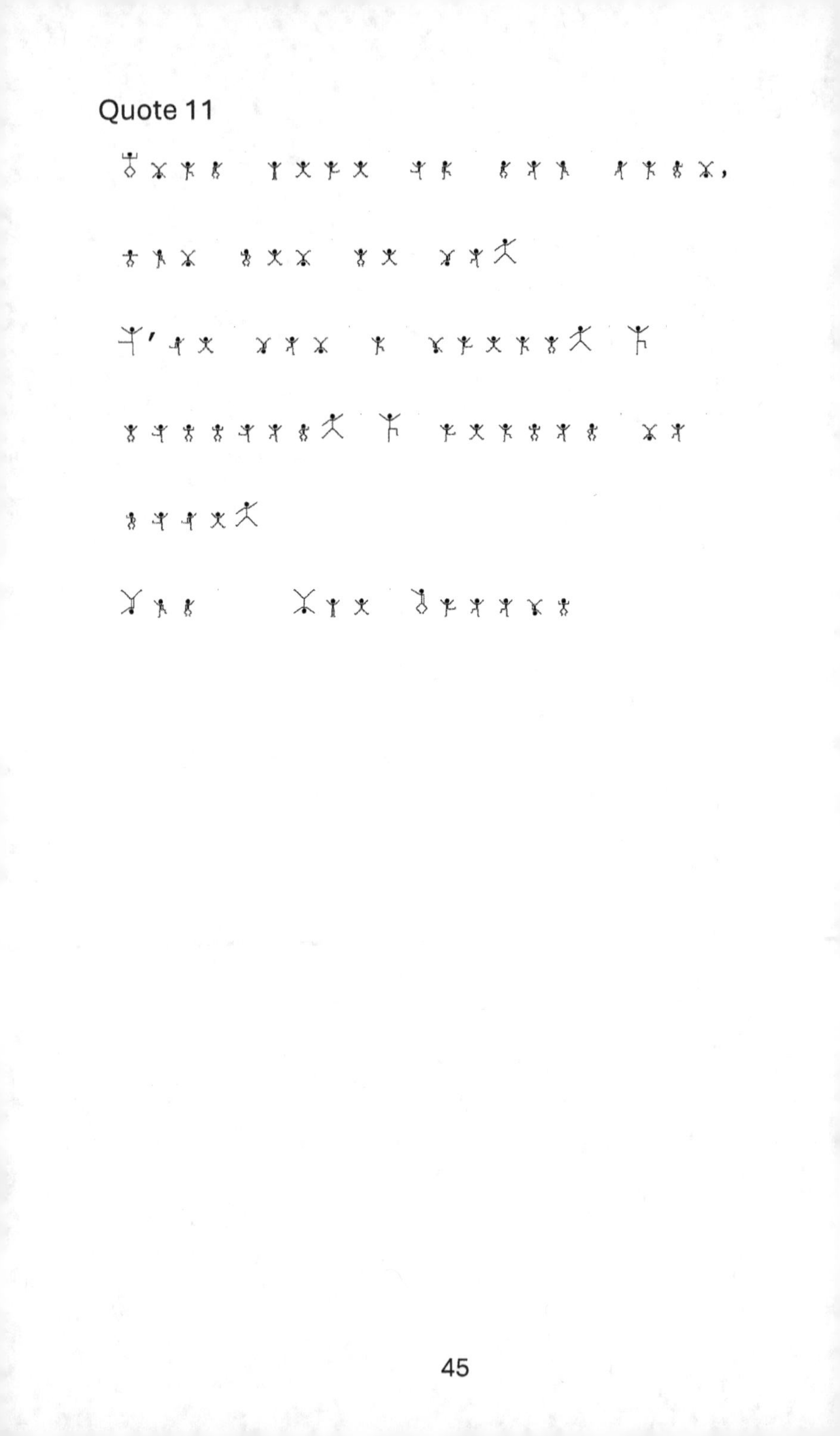

Quote 11

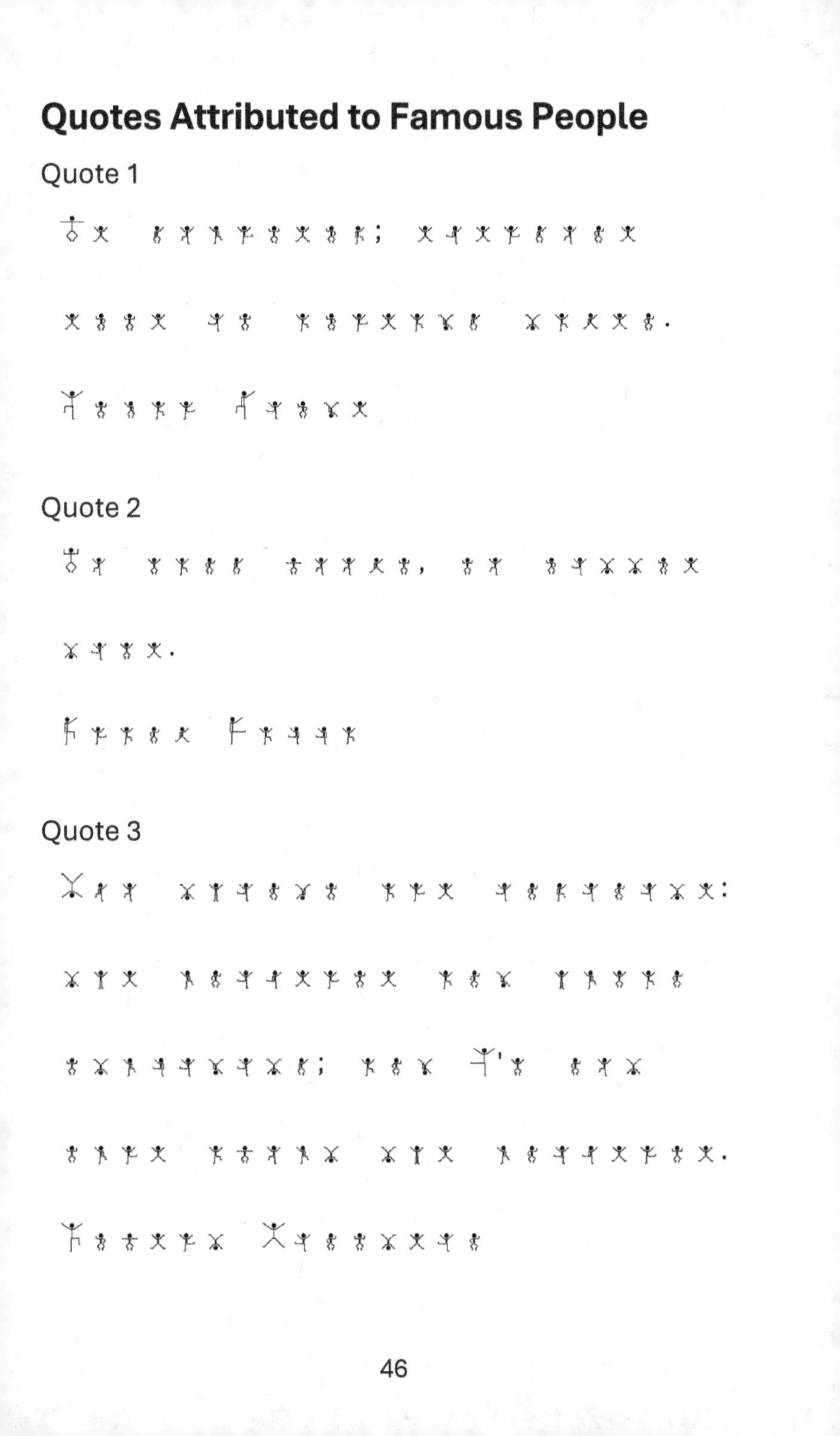

Quotes Attributed to Famous People

Quote 1

Quote 2

Quote 3

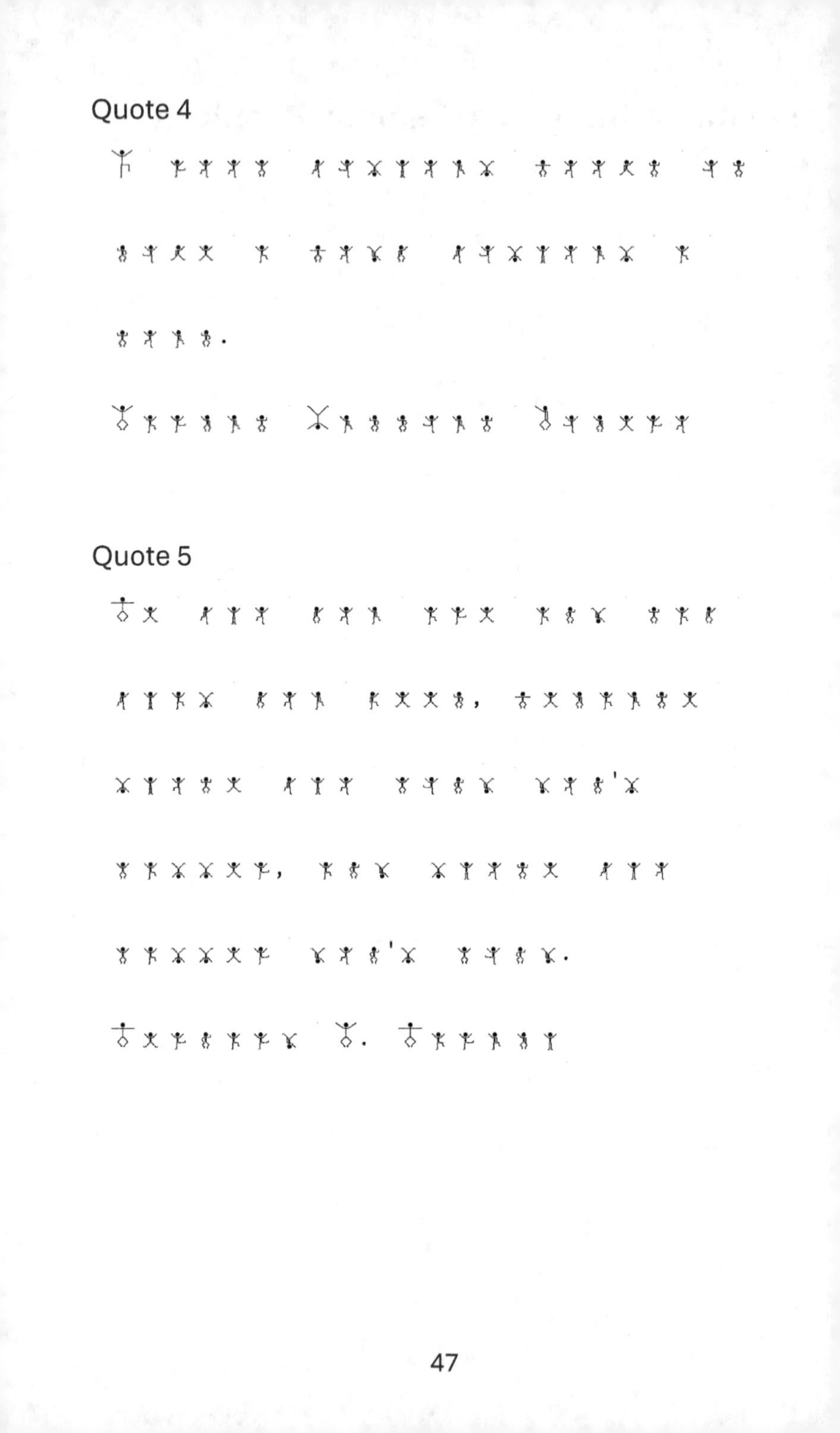

Quote 4

Quote 5

Quote 6

Quote 7

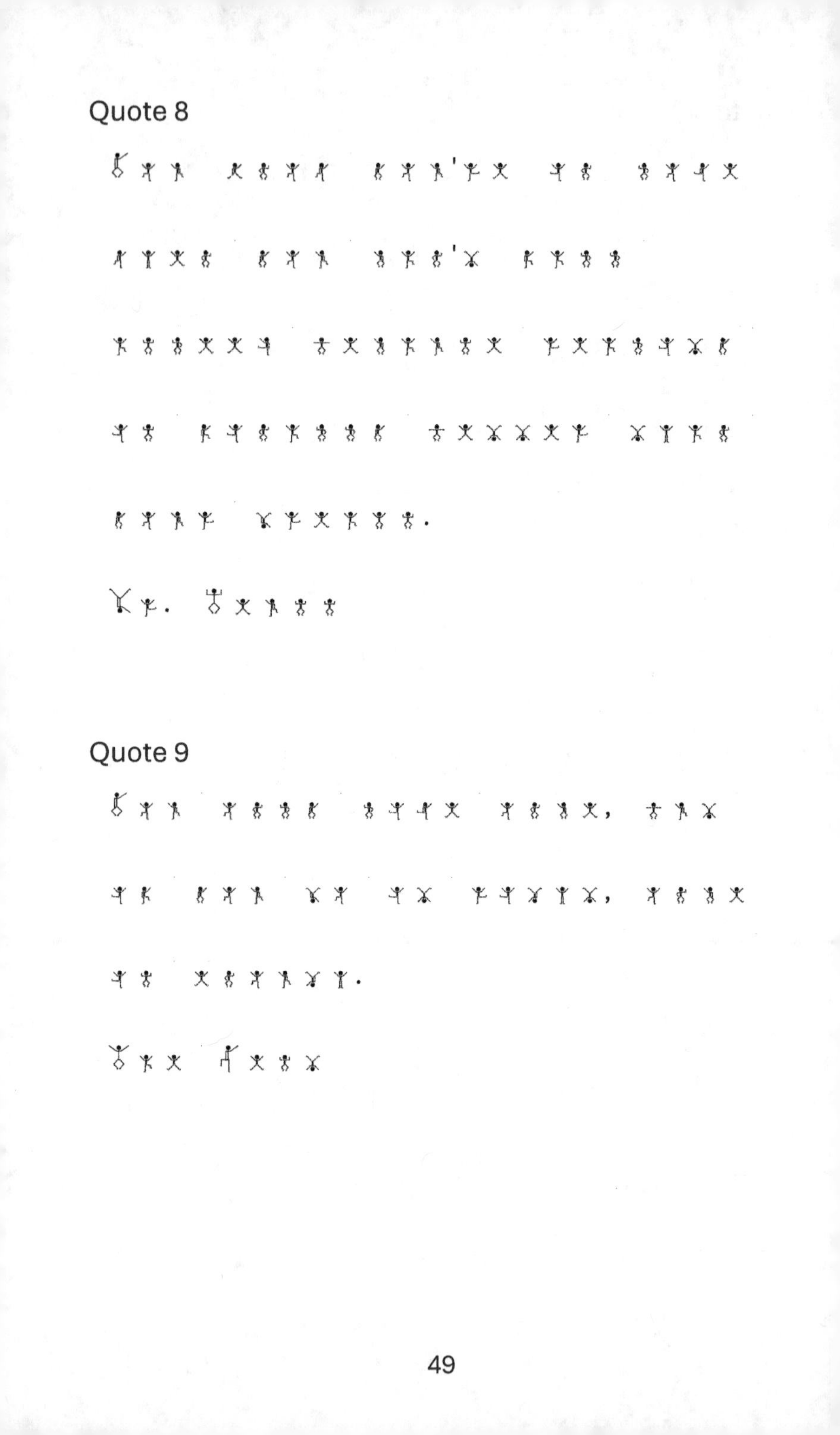

Quote 8

Quote 9

Quote 10

Quote 11

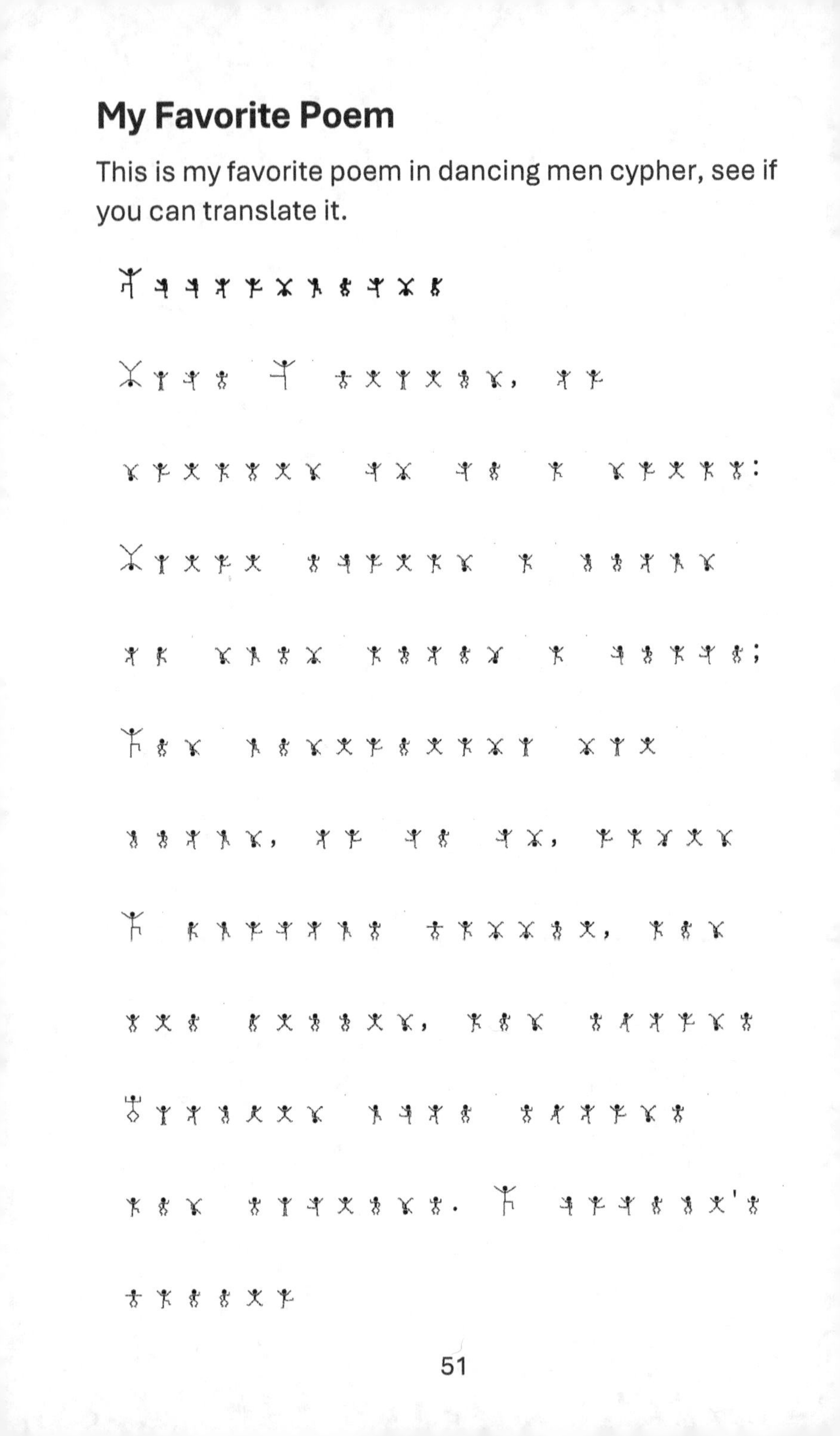

My Favorite Poem

This is my favorite poem in dancing men cypher, see if you can translate it.

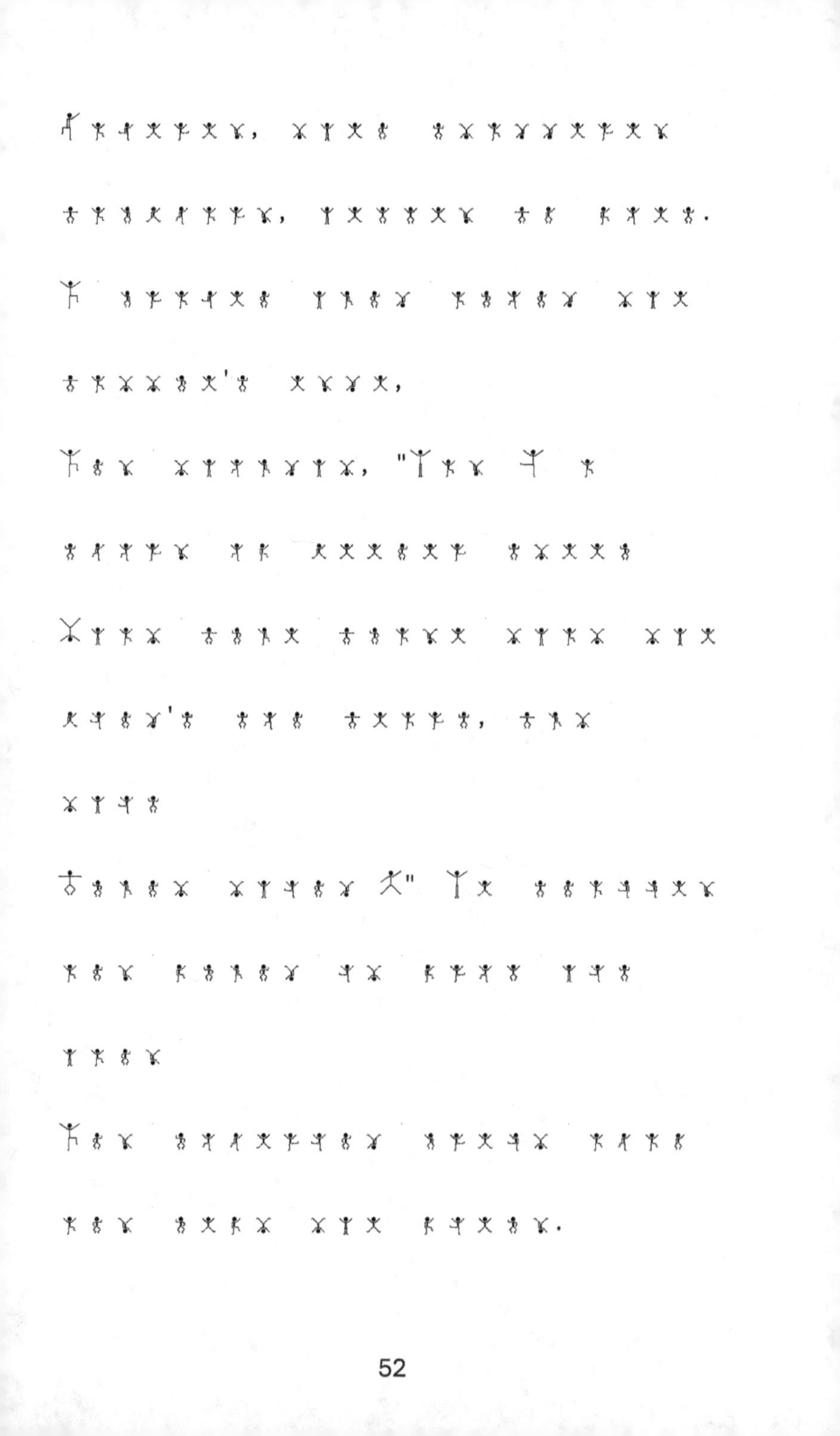

Combining With Other Codes

The Easter Basket Cypher

This is a multi-layered cypher that I created for my kids for Easter in 2021. They had to solve this to figure out where their Easter baskets were. It took them four hours! I did not mean to make it that hard. They were tired by the end but had fun. It combines a dancing men cypher, book cypher, numeric cypher, and a riddle.

Dancing Man Morse Code

Morse code was developed in the 1800s for telegraphy. It is only reliant on two distinct signals called "dit" represented by a dot and "dah" represented by a dash. While telegraphy is not used much today, morse code is still used by Ham radio operators and in some military situations. This is what it looks like.

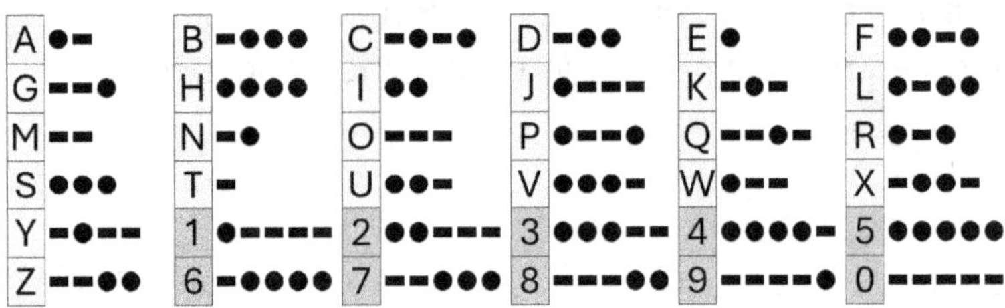

A •—	B —•••	C —•—•	D —••	E •	F ••—•
G ——•	H ••••	I ••	J •———	K —•—	L •—••
M ——	N —•	O ———	P •——•	Q ——•—	R •—•
S •••	T —	U ••—	V •••—	W •——	X —••—
Y —•——	1 •————	2 ••———	3 •••——	4 ••••—	5 •••••
Z ——••	6 —••••	7 ——•••	8 ———••	9 ————•	0 —————

I always thought it would be fun to combine morse code and the dancing men font. We could reduce it down to just the letters A (dah) and I (dit) (𝍢 and 𝍣). The difference between the two is just right leg and left leg. This is something that could be communicated visually from a distance. Below shows the combined dancing men Morse code.

My Dream For the Future

It was the use of the dancing men cypher with my kids that led me to a new vision of how I might use fun code going forward. Fifteen years ago, I wrote my first Children's Book, One-Eyed Same and the Purple Pillow. I probably sold 30 copies. Then life happened, priorities changed, I let fear rule the day, and stopped writing, stopped drawing, stopped creating. It took me a while to bounce back from that, but that is a story for another day. The point to remember is that I did bounce back, and it started in 2020. That year changed everything.

My favorite quote from that year came from Steven Spielberg. That man may never know how much he has affected my life. It is on my bucket list to meet him someday so I can tell him face to face. He said, "the one thing we learned from Covid, is that anything is possible and that means, anything is possible! Isn't that exciting." That idea grew in me. I started carving river rocks and created a whole brand called HappyRocks. This past November, I rediscovered the world of self-publishing thanks to the Mikkelsen twins.

I wanted to restart my book publishing with a relaunch of my book from over a decade ago, but I wanted to create something bigger than just one great kids book.

When I was a kid, I used to see these cool western paintings by the artist Bev Doolittle. She employes an artistic method that she calls camouflage art. As her website says, she is "one of America's most collected artists." A friend of mine who is an accomplished illustrator told me that he and his colleagues referred to Doolittle's success as the Doolittle Phenomenon. You really need to look at her art to see why she has captivated people so much, but when I say look, I mean it. If you just glance at her work, you will miss the magic. Her art is layered. When viewed one way it will look like one thing and then suddenly you will see something else. Brilliant! Thinking about her made me consider the possibility of doing something like that in my books. What if I could tell more than one story at once or at least provide more context to the story that is there?

So I took my 13-year-old book, gave it a much better cover, and then wrote a short commentary for it. I thought of my Happy Rocks. What would they say if they read the book? How would they react? I then converted that commentary into the dancing men cypher. Its scattered throughout the book. Going forward it will be present in every single book I write. It is like a form of camouflage writing.

I love these silly little dancing figures and find myself constantly thinking about how to use them more, and how to help everyone know them and love them too. I suppose that the real dream is that they graduate from being a cypher, something hard to understand to just another font with presence everywhere; clothes, dances, movies, hats... the ideas are near infinite. We will just have to wait and see how it all develops.

Extras

The Original Sherlock Holmes story

Below is the original Sherlock Holmes story where the dancing men cypher first appeared. I can make it available here because thanks to a ruling on the legal case, *Klinger v. Conan Doyle Estate*, Sherlock Holms is officially part of the open domain. While we provide this single story here because of its relationship with the Dancing Men cypher, I encourage everyone to go out and buy your own copy of the complete Sherlock Holmes stories. There are some beautiful printings now available, and the stories are well worth the read.

The Adventure of the Dancing Men

By Arthur Conan Doyle

Holmes had been seated for some hours in silence with his long, thin back curved over a chemical vessel in which he was brewing a particularly malodorous product. His head was sunk upon his breast, and he looked from my point of view like a strange, lank bird, with dull grey plumage and a black top-knot.

"So, Watson," said he, suddenly, "you do not propose to invest in South African securities?"

I gave a start of astonishment. Accustomed as I was to Holmes's curious faculties, this sudden intrusion into my most intimate thoughts was utterly inexplicable.

"How on earth do you know that?" I asked. He wheeled round upon his stool, with a steaming test-tube in his hand and a gleam of amusement in his deep-set eyes.

"Now, Watson, confess yourself utterly taken aback," said he.

"I am."

"I ought to make you sign a paper to that effect."

"Why?"

"Because in five minutes you will say that it is all so absurdly simple."

"I am sure that I shall say nothing of the kind."

"You see, my dear Watson"—he propped his test-tube in the rack and began to lecture with the air of a professor addressing his class—"it is not re- ally difficult to construct a series of inferences, each dependent upon its predecessor and each simple in itself. If, after doing so, one simply knocks out all the central inferences and presents one's audience with the starting-point and the conclusion, one may produce a startling, though possibly a meretricious, effect. Now, it was not really difficult, by an inspection of the groove between your left forefinger and thumb, to feel sure that you did not propose to invest your small capital in the goldfields."

"I see no connection."

"Very likely not; but I can quickly show you a close connection. Here are the missing links of the very simple chain: 1. You had chalk between your left finger and thumb when you returned from the club last night. 2. You put chalk there when you play billiards to steady the cue. 3. You never play billiards except with Thurston. 4. You told me four weeks ago that Thurston had an option on some South African property which would expire in a month, and which he desired you to share with him. 5. Your cheque-book is locked in my drawer, and you have not asked for the key. 6. You do not propose to invest your money in this manner."

"How absurdly simple!" I cried.

"Quite so!" said he, a little nettled. "Every problem becomes very childish when once it is explained to you.

Here is an unexplained one. See what you can make of that, friend Watson." He tossed a sheet of paper upon the table and turned once more to his chemical analysis.

I looked with amazement at the absurd hieroglyphics upon the paper.

"Why, Holmes, it is a child's drawing," I cried. "Oh, that's your idea!"

"What else should it be?"

"That is what Mr. Hilton Cubitt, of Ridling Thorpe Manor, Norfolk, is very anxious to know. This little conundrum came by the first post, and he was to follow by the next train. There's a ring at the bell, Watson. I should not be very much surprised if this were he."

A heavy step was heard upon the stairs, and an instant later there entered a tall, ruddy, clean- shaven gentleman, whose clear eyes and florid cheeks told of a life led far from the fogs of Baker Street. He seemed to bring a whiff of his strong, fresh, bracing, east-coast air with him as he entered. Having shaken hands with each of us, he was about to sit down when his eye rested upon the paper with the curious markings, which I had just examined and left upon the table.

"Well, Mr. Holmes, what do you make of these?" he cried. "They told me that you were fond of queer mysteries, and I don't think you can find a queerer one than that. I sent the paper on ahead so that you might have time to study it before I came."

"It is certainly rather a curious production," said Holmes. "At first sight it would appear to be some childish prank. It consists of a number of absurd little figures dancing across the paper upon which they are drawn. Why should you attribute any importance to so grotesque an object?"

"I never should, Mr. Holmes. But my wife does. It is frightening her to death. She says nothing, but I can see terror in her eyes. That's why I want to sift the matter to the bottom."

Holmes held up the paper so that the sunlight shone full upon it. It was a page torn from a note- book. The markings were done in pencil, and ran in this way:

Holmes examined it for some time, and then, folding it carefully up, he placed it in his pocket- book.

"This promises to be a most interesting and un- usual case," said he. "You gave me a few particulars in your letter, Mr. Hilton Cubitt, but I should be very much obliged if you would kindly go over it all again for the benefit of my friend, Dr. Watson."

"I'm not much of a story-teller," said our visitor, nervously clasping and unclasping his great, strong hands. "You'll just ask me anything that I don't make clear. I'll begin at the time of my marriage last year; but I want to say first of all that, though I'm not a rich man, my people have been at Ridling Thorpe for a matter of five centuries, and there is no better-known family in the County of Norfolk. Last year I came up to London for the Jubilee, and I stopped at a boarding-house in Russell Square, because Parker, the vicar of our parish, was staying in it. There was an American young lady there—Patrick was the name—Elsie Patrick. In some way we became friends, until before my month was up I was as much in love as a man could be. We were quietly married at a registry office, and we returned to Norfolk a wedded couple. You'll think it very mad, Mr. Holmes, that a man of a good old family should marry a wife in this fashion, knowing nothing of her past or of her people; but if you saw her and knew her it would help you to understand.

"She was very straight about it, was Elsie. I can't say that she did not give me every chance of getting out of it if I wished to do so. 'I have had some very disagreeable associations in my life,' said she; 'I wish to forget all about them. I would rather never allude to the past, for it is very painful to me. If you take me, Hilton, you will take a woman who has nothing that she need be personally ashamed of; but you will have to be content with my word for it, and to allow me to be silent as to all that passed up to the time when I became yours. If these conditions are too hard, then go back to Norfolk and leave me to the lonely life in which you found me.' It was only the day before our wedding that she said those very words to me. I told her that I was content to take her on her own terms, and I have been as good as my word.

"Well, we have been married now for a year, and very happy we have been. But about a month ago, at the end of June, I saw for the first-time signs of trouble. One day my wife received a letter from America. I saw the American stamp. She turned deadly white, read the letter, and threw it into the fire. She made no allusion to it afterwards, and I made none, for a promise is a promise; but she has never known an easy hour from that moment. There is always a look of fear upon her face—a look as if she were waiting and expecting. She would do better to trust me. She would find that I was her best friend. But until she speaks I can say nothing. Mind you, she is a truthful woman, Mr. Holmes, and whatever trouble there may have been in her past life it has been no fault of hers. I am only a simple Norfolk squire, but there is not a man in England who ranks his family honour more highly than I do. She knows it well, and she knew it well before she married me. She would never bring any stain upon it—of that I am sure.

"Well, now I come to the queer part of my story. About a week ago—it was the Tuesday of last week—I found on one of the window-sills a number of absurd little dancing figures, like these upon the paper. They were scrawled with chalk. I thought that it was the stable-boy who had drawn them, but the lad swore he knew nothing about it. Anyhow, they had come there during the night. I had them washed out, and I only mentioned the matter to my wife afterwards. To my surprise she took it very seriously, and begged me if any more came to let her see them. None did come for a week, and then yesterday morning I found this pa- per lying on the sun-dial in the garden. I showed it to Elsie, and down she dropped in a dead faint. Since then she has looked like a woman in a dream, half dazed, and with terror always lurking in her eyes. It was then that I wrote and sent the paper to you, Mr. Holmes. It was not a thing that I could take to the police, for they would have laughed at me, but you will tell me what to do. I am not a rich man; but if there is any danger threatening my little woman I would spend my last copper to shield her."

He was a fine creature, this man of the old English soil, simple, straight, and gentle, with his great, earnest blue eyes and broad, comely face. His love for his wife and his trust in her shone in his features. Holmes had listened to his story with the utmost attention, and now he sat for some time in silent thought.

"Don't you think, Mr. Cubitt," said he, at last, "that your best plan would be to make a direct ap- peal to your wife, and to ask her to share her secret with you?"

Hilton Cubitt shook his massive head.

"A promise is a promise, Mr. Holmes. If Elsie wished to tell me she would. If not, it is not for me to force her confidence. But I am justified in taking my own line— and I will."

"Then I will help you with all my heart. In the first place, have you heard of any strangers being seen in your neighbourhood?"

"No."

"I presume that it is a very quiet place. Any fresh face would cause comment?"

"In the immediate neighbourhood, yes. But we have several small watering-places not very far away. And the farmers take in lodgers."

"These hieroglyphics have evidently a meaning. If it is a purely arbitrary one it may be impossible for us to solve it. If, on the other hand, it is systematic, I have no doubt that we shall get to the bottom of it. But this particular sample is so short that I can do nothing, and the facts which you have brought me are so indefinite that we have no basis for an investigation. I would suggest that you return to Norfolk, that you keep a keen look-out, and that you take an exact copy of any fresh dancing men which may appear. It is a thousand pities that we have not a reproduction of those which were done in chalk upon the window-sill. Make a discreet inquiry also as to any strangers in the neighbourhood. When you have collected some fresh evidence come to me again. That is the best advice which I can give you, Mr. Hilton Cubitt. If there are any pressing fresh developments I shall be always ready to run down and see you in your Norfolk home."

The interview left Sherlock Holmes very thoughtful, and several times in the next few days I saw him take his slip of paper from his note-book and look long and earnestly at the curious figures inscribed upon it. He made no allusion to the affair, however, until one afternoon a fortnight or so later. I was going out when he called me back.

"You had better stay here, Watson." "Why?"

"Because I had a wire from Hilton Cubitt this morning—you remember Hilton Cubitt, of the dancing men? He was to reach Liverpool Street at one-twenty. He may be here at any moment. I gather from his wire that there have been some new incidents of importance."

We had not long to wait, for our Norfolk squire came straight from the station as fast as a hansom could bring him. He was looking worried and depressed, with tired eyes and a lined forehead.

"It's getting on my nerves, this business, Mr. Holmes," said he, as he sank, like a wearied man, into an arm-chair. "It's bad enough to feel that you are surrounded by unseen, unknown folk, who have some kind of design upon you; but when, in addition to that, you know that it is just killing your wife by inches, then it becomes as much as flesh and blood can endure. She's wearing away under it—just wearing away before my eyes."

"Has she said anything yet?"

"No, Mr. Holmes, she has not. And yet there have been times when the poor girl has wanted to speak, and yet could not quite bring herself to take the plunge. I have tried to help her; but I dare say I did it clumsily, and scared her off from it. She has spoken about my old family, and our reputation in the county, and our pride in our unsullied honour, and I always felt it was leading to the point; but somehow it turned off before we got there."

"But you have found out something for your- self?"

"A good deal, Mr. Holmes. I have several fresh dancing men pictures for you to examine, and, what is more important, I have seen the fellow."

"What, the man who draws them?"

"Yes, I saw him at his work. But I will tell you everything in order. When I got back after my visit to you, the very first thing I saw next morning was a fresh crop of dancing men. They had been drawn in chalk upon the black wooden door of the tool- house, which stands beside the lawn in full view of the front windows. I took an exact copy, and here it is." He unfolded a paper and laid it upon the table. Here is a copy of the hieroglyphics:

"Excellent!" said Holmes. "Excellent! Pray continue."

"When I had taken the copy I rubbed out the marks; but two mornings later a fresh inscription had appeared. I have a copy of it here":

Holmes rubbed his hands and chuckled with delight.

"Our material is rapidly accumulating," said he. "Three days later a message was left scrawled upon paper, and placed under a pebble upon the

sun-dial. Here it is. The characters are, as you see,

exactly the same as the last one. After that I deter-
mined to lie in wait; so I got out my revolver and I sat up
in my study, which overlooks the lawn and garden.
About two in the morning I was seated by the window,
all being dark save for the moonlight outside, when I
heard steps behind me, and there was my wife in her
dressing-gown. She implored me to come to bed. I told
her frankly that I wished to see who it was who played
such absurd tricks upon us. She answered that it was
some senseless practical joke, and that I should not
take any notice of it.

" 'If it really annoys you, Hilton, we might go and travel,
you and I, and so avoid this nuisance.'

" 'What, be driven out of our own house by a practical
joker?' said I. 'Why, we should have the whole county
laughing at us.'

" 'Well, come to bed,' said she, 'and we can discuss it
in the morning.'

"Suddenly, as she spoke, I saw her white face grow
whiter yet in the moonlight, and her hand tightened
upon my shoulder. Something was moving in the
shadow of the tool-house. I saw a dark, creeping figure
which crawled round the corner and squatted in front of
the door. Seizing my pistol I was rushing out, when my
wife threw her arms round me and held me with
convulsive strength. I tried to throw her off, but she
clung to me most desperately. At last I got clear, but by
the time I had opened the door and reached the house
the creature was gone. He had left a trace of his

presence, however, for there on the door was the very same arrangement of dancing men which had al- ready twice appeared, and which I have copied on that paper. There was no other sign of the fellow anywhere, though I ran all over the grounds. And yet the amazing thing is that he must have been there all the time, for when I examined the door again in the morning he had scrawled some more of his pictures under the line which I had already seen.”

“Have you that fresh drawing?”

“Yes; it is very short, but I made a copy of it, and here it is.”

Again he produced a paper. The new dance was in this form:

“Tell me,” said Holmes—and I could see by his eyes that he was much excited—“was this a mere addition to the first, or did it appear to be entirely separate?”

“It was on a different panel of the door.” “Excellent! This is far the most important of all for our purpose. It fills me with hopes. Now, Mr. Hilton Cubitt, please continue your most interesting statement.”

“I have nothing more to say, Mr. Holmes, except that I was angry with my wife that night for having held me back when I might have caught the skulking rascal. She said that she feared that I might come to harm. For an instant it had crossed my mind that perhaps what she really feared was that he might come to harm, for I could not doubt that she knew who this man was and what he meant by these strange signals. But there is a tone in my wife's voice, Mr. Holmes, and a look in her eyes which forbid doubt, and I am sure that it was indeed my own safety that was in her mind. There's the whole case, and now I want your advice as to what I ought to do. My own inclination is to put half-a-dozen of my farm lads in the shrubbery, and when this fellow comes again to give him such a hiding that he will leave us in peace for the future." "I fear it is too deep a case for such simple remedies," said Holmes. "How long can you stay in London?"

"I must go back to-day. I would not leave my wife alone all night for anything. She is very nervous and begged me to come back."

"I dare say you are right. But if you could have stopped I might possibly have been able to return with you in a day or two. Meanwhile you will leave me these papers, and I think that it is very likely that I shall be able to pay you a visit shortly and to throw some light upon your case."

Sherlock Holmes preserved his calm professional manner until our visitor had left us, although it was easy for me, who knew him so well, to see that he was profoundly excited. The moment that Hilton Cubitt's broad back had disappeared through the door my comrade rushed to the table, laid out all the slips of paper containing dancing men in front of him, and threw himself into an intricate and elaborate calculation. For two hours I watched him as he covered sheet after sheet of paper with figures and letters, so completely absorbed in his task that he had evidently forgotten my presence. Sometimes he was making progress and whistled and sang at his work; sometimes he was puzzled, and would sit for long spells with a furrowed brow and a vacant eye. Finally he sprang from his chair with a cry of satisfaction, and walked up and down the room rubbing his hands together. Then he wrote a long telegram upon a cable form. "If my answer to this is as I hope, you will have a very pretty case to add to your collection, Wat- son," said he. "I expect that we shall be able to go down to Norfolk to-morrow, and to take our friend some very definite news as to the secret of his annoyance."

I confess that I was filled with curiosity, but I was aware that Holmes liked to make his disclosures at his own time and in his own way; so I waited until it should suit him to take me into his confidence.

But there was a delay in that answering tele- gram, and two days of impatience followed, during which Holmes pricked up his ears at every ring of the bell. On the evening of the second there came a letter from Hilton Cubitt. All was quiet with him, save that a long inscription had appeared that morning upon the pedestal of the sun-dial. He inclosed a copy of it, which is here reproduced:

Holmes bent over this grotesque frieze for some minutes, and then suddenly sprang to his feet with an exclamation of surprise and dismay. His face was haggard with anxiety.

"We have let this affair go far enough," said he. "Is there a train to North Walsham to-night?"

I turned up the time-table. The last had just gone.

"Then we shall breakfast early and take the very first in the morning," said Holmes. "Our presence is most urgently needed. Ah! here is our expected cablegram. One moment, Mrs. Hudson; there may be an answer. No, that is quite as I expected. This message makes it even more essential that we should not lose an hour in letting Hilton Cubitt know how matters stand, for it is a singular and a dangerous web in which our simple Norfolk squire is entangled."

So, indeed, it proved, and as I come to the dark conclusion of a story which had seemed to me to be only childish and bizarre I experience once again the dismay and horror with which I was filled. Would that I had some brighter ending to communicate to my readers, but these are the chronicles of fact, and I must follow to their dark crisis the strange chain of events which for some days made Ridling Thorpe Manor a household word through the length and breadth of England.

We had hardly alighted at North Walsham, and mentioned the name of our destination, when the station-master hurried towards us. "I suppose that you are the detectives from London?" said he.

A look of annoyance passed over Holmes's face. "What makes you think such a thing?" "Because Inspector Martin from Norwich has

just passed through. But maybe you are the surgeons. She's not dead—or wasn't by last accounts. You may be in time to save her yet—though it be for the gallows."

Holmes's brow was dark with anxiety.

"We are going to Ridling Thorpe Manor," said he, "but we have heard nothing of what has passed there."

"It's a terrible business," said the station-master. "They are shot, both Mr. Hilton Cubitt and his wife. She shot him and then herself—so the servants say. He's dead and her life is despaired of. Dear, dear, one of the oldest families in the County of Norfolk, and one of the most honoured."

Without a word Holmes hurried to a carriage, and during the long seven miles' drive he never opened his mouth. Seldom have I seen him so utterly despondent. He had been uneasy during all our journey from town, and I had observed that he had turned over the morning papers with anxious attention; but now this sudden realization of his worst fears left him in a blank melancholy. He leaned back in his seat, lost in gloomy speculation. Yet there was much around to interest us, for we were passing through as singular a country-side as any in England, where a few scattered cottages represented the population of to-day, while on every hand enormous square-towered churches bristled up from the flat, green landscape and told of the glory and prosperity of old East Anglia. At last the violet rim of the German Ocean appeared over the green edge of the Norfolk coast, and the driver pointed with his whip to two old brick and timber gables which projected from a grove of trees. "That's Ridling Thorpe Manor," said he.

As we drove up to the porticoed front door I observed in front of it, beside the tennis lawn, the black tool-house and the pedestalled sun-dial with which we had such strange associations. A dapper little man, with a quick, alert manner and a waxed moustache, had just descended from a high dog- cart. He introduced himself as Inspector Martin, of the Norfolk Constabulary, and he was considerably astonished when he heard the name of my companion.

"Why, Mr. Holmes, the crime was only commit- ted at three this morning. How could you hear of it in London and get to the spot as soon as I?"

"I anticipated it. I came in the hope of preventing it."

"Then you must have important evidence of which we are ignorant, for they were said to be a most united couple."

"I have only the evidence of the dancing men," said Holmes. "I will explain the matter to you later. Meanwhile, since it is too late to prevent this tragedy, I am very anxious that I should use the knowledge which I possess in order to ensure that justice be done. Will you associate me in your investigation, or will you prefer that I should act independently?”

“I should be proud to feel that we were acting together, Mr. Holmes,” said the inspector, earnestly.

“In that case I should be glad to hear the evidence and to examine the premises without an instant of unnecessary delay.”

Inspector Martin had the good sense to allow my friend to do things in his own fashion, and contented himself with carefully noting the results. The local surgeon, an old, white-haired man, had just come down from Mrs. Hilton Cubitt’s room, and he reported that her injuries were serious, but not necessarily fatal. The bullet had passed through the front of her brain, and it would probably be some time before she could regain consciousness. On the question of whether she had been shot or had shot herself he would not venture to express any decided opinion. Certainly the bullet had been discharged at very close quarters. There was only the one pistol found in the room, two barrels of which had been emptied. Mr. Hilton Cubitt had been shot through the heart. It was equally conceivable that he had shot her and then himself, or that she had been the criminal, for the revolver lay upon the floor midway between them.

“Has he been moved?” asked Holmes.

“We have moved nothing except the lady. We could not leave her lying wounded upon the floor.”

"How long have you been here, doctor?" "Since four o'clock."

"Anyone else?"

"Yes, the constable here."

"And you have touched nothing?" "Nothing."

"You have acted with great discretion. Who sent for you?"

"The housemaid, Saunders." "Was it she who gave the alarm?" "She and Mrs. King, the cook." "Where are they now?"

"In the kitchen, I believe."

"Then I think we had better hear their story at once."

The old hall, oak-panelled and high-windowed, had been turned into a court of investigation. Holmes sat in a great, old-fashioned chair, his in- exorable eyes gleaming out of his haggard face. I could read in them a set purpose to devote his life to this quest until the client whom he had failed to save should at last be avenged. The trim Inspector Martin, the old, grey-headed country doctor, my- self, and a stolid village policeman made up the rest of that strange company.

The two women told their story clearly enough. They had been aroused from their sleep by the sound of an explosion, which had been followed a minute later by a second one. They slept in ad- joining rooms, and Mrs. King had rushed in to Saunders. Together they had descended the stairs. The door of the study was open and a candle was burning upon the table. Their master lay upon his face in the centre of the room. He was quite dead. Near the window his wife was crouching, her head leaning against the wall. She was horribly wounded, and the side of her face was red with blood. She breathed heavily, but was incapable of saying anything. The passage, as well as the room, was full of smoke and the smell of powder. The window was certainly shut and fastened upon the inside. Both women were positive upon the point. They had at once sent for the doctor and for the constable. Then, with the aid of the groom and the stable-boy, they had conveyed their injured mis- tress to her room. Both she and her husband had occupied the bed. She was clad in her dress—he in his dressing-gown, over his night clothes. Nothing had been moved in the study. So far as they knew there had never been any quarrel between husband and wife. They had always looked upon them as a very united couple.

These were the main points of the servants' evidence. In answer to Inspector Martin they were clear that every door was fastened upon the inside, and that no one could have escaped from the house. In answer to Holmes they both remembered that they were conscious of the smell of powder from the moment that they ran out of their rooms upon the top floor. "I commend that fact very carefully to your attention," said Holmes to his professional colleague. "And now I think that we are in a position to undertake a thorough examination of the room."

The study proved to be a small chamber, lined on three sides with books, and with a writing-table facing an ordinary window, which looked out upon the garden. Our first attention was given to the body of the unfortunate squire, whose huge frame lay stretched across the room. His disordered dress showed that he had been hastily aroused from sleep. The bullet had been fired at him from the front, and had remained in his body after penetrating the heart. His death had certainly been instantaneous and painless. There was no powder-marking either upon his dressing-gown or on his hands. According to the country surgeon the lady had stains upon her face, but none upon her hand.

"The absence of the latter means nothing, though its presence may mean everything," said Holmes. "Unless the powder from a badly-fitting cartridge happens to spurt backwards, one may fire many shots without leaving a sign. I would suggest that Mr. Cubitt's body may now be removed. I suppose, doctor, you have not recovered the bullet which wounded the lady?"

"A serious operation will be necessary before that can be done. But there are still four cartridges in the revolver. Two have been fired and two wounds inflicted, so that each bullet can be ac- counted for."

"So it would seem," said Holmes. "Perhaps you can account also for the bullet which has so obviously struck the edge of the window?"

He had turned suddenly, and his long, thin fin- ger was pointing to a hole which had been drilled right through the lower window-sash about an inch above the bottom.

"By George!" cried the inspector. "How ever did you see that?"

"Because I looked for it."

"Wonderful!" said the country doctor. "You are certainly right, sir. Then a third shot has been fired, and therefore a third person must have been present. But who could that have been and how could he have got away?"

"That is the problem which we are now about to solve," said Sherlock Holmes. "You remember, Inspector Martin, when the servants said that on leaving their room they were at once conscious of a smell of powder I remarked that the point was an extremely important one?"

"Yes, sir; but I confess I did not quite follow you."

"It suggested that at the time of the firing the window as well as the door of the room had been open. Otherwise the fumes of powder could not have been blown so rapidly through the house. A draught in the room was necessary for that. Both door and window were only open for a very short time, however."

"How do you prove that?"

"Because the candle has not guttered." "Capital!" cried the inspector. "Capital!" "Feeling sure that the window had been open at the time of the tragedy I conceived that there might have been a third person in the affair, who stood outside this opening and fired through it. Any shot directed at this person might hit the sash. I looked, and there, sure enough, was the bullet mark!"

"But how came the window to be shut and fastened?"

"The woman's first instinct would be to shut and fasten the window. But, halloa! what is this?"

It was a lady's hand-bag which stood upon the study table—a trim little hand-bag of crocodile-skin and silver. Holmes opened it and turned the con- tents out. There were twenty fifty-pound notes of the Bank of England, held together by an India- rubber band—nothing else.

"This must be preserved, for it will figure in the trial," said Holmes, as he handed the bag with its contents to the inspector. "It is now necessary that we should try to throw some light upon this third bullet, which has clearly, from the splintering of the wood, been fired from inside the room. I should like to see Mrs. King, the cook, again. You said, Mrs. King, that you were awakened by a loud explosion. When you said that, did you mean that it seemed to you to be louder than the second one?"

"Well, sir, it wakened me from my sleep, and so it is hard to judge. But it did seem very loud."

"You don't think that it might have been two shots fired almost at the same instant?"

"I am sure I couldn't say, sir."

"I believe that it was undoubtedly so. I rather think, Inspector Martin, that we have now exhausted all that this room can teach us. If you will kindly step round with me, we shall see what fresh evidence the garden has to offer."

A flower-bed extended up to the study window, and we all broke into an exclamation as we approached it. The flowers were trampled down, and the soft soil was imprinted all over with footmarks. Large, masculine feet they were, with peculiarly long, sharp toes. Holmes hunted about among the grass and leaves like a retriever after a wounded bird. Then, with a cry of satisfaction, he bent for- ward and picked up a little brazen cylinder.

"I thought so," said he; "the revolver had an ejector, and here is the third cartridge. I really think, Inspector Martin, that our case is almost complete."

The country inspector's face had shown his intense amazement at the rapid and masterful progress of Holmes's investigation. At first he had shown some disposition to assert his own position; but now he was overcome with admiration and ready to follow without question wherever Holmes led.

"Whom do you suspect?" he asked.

"I'll go into that later. There are several points in this problem which I have not been able to ex- plain to you yet. Now that I have got so far I had best proceed on my own lines, and then clear the whole matter up once and for all.”

“Just as you wish, Mr. Holmes, so long as we get our man.”

“I have no desire to make mysteries, but it is impossible at the moment of action to enter into long and complex explanations. I have the threads of this affair all in my hand. Even if this lady should never recover consciousness we can still re- construct the events of last night and ensure that justice be done. First of all I wish to know whether there is any inn in this neighbourhood known as ‘Elrige’s’?”

The servants were cross-questioned, but none of them had heard of such a place. The stable-boy threw a light upon the matter by remembering that a farmer of that name lived some miles off in the direction of East Ruston.

“Is it a lonely farm?” “Very lonely, sir.”

“Perhaps they have not heard yet of all that happened here during the night?”

“Maybe not, sir.”

Holmes thought for a little and then a curious smile played over his face.

“Saddle a horse, my lad,” said he. “I shall wish you to take a note to Elrige’s Farm.”

He took from his pocket the various slips of the dancing men. With these in front of him he worked for some time at the study-table. Finally he handed a note to the boy, with directions to put it into the hands of the person to whom it was addressed, and especially to answer no questions of any sort which might be put to him. I saw the outside of the note, addressed in straggling, irregular characters, very unlike Holmes's usual precise hand. It was consigned to Mr. Abe Slaney, Elrige's Farm, East Ruston, Norfolk.

"I think, inspector," Holmes remarked, "that you would do well to telegraph for an escort, as, if my calculations prove to be correct, you may have a particularly dangerous prisoner to convey to the county jail. The boy who takes this note could no doubt forward your telegram. If there is an afternoon train to town, Watson, I think we should do well to take it, as I have a chemical analysis of some interest to finish, and this investigation draws rapidly to a close."

When the youth had been dispatched with the note, Sherlock Holmes gave his instructions to the servants. If any visitor were to call asking for Mrs. Hilton Cubitt no information should be given as to her condition, but he was to be shown at once into the drawing-room. He impressed these points upon them with the utmost earnestness. Finally he led the way into the drawing-room with the remark that the business was now out of our hands, and that we must while away the time as best we might until we could see what was in store for us. The doctor had departed to his patients, and only the inspector and myself remained.

"I think that I can help you to pass an hour in an interesting and profitable manner," said Holmes, drawing his chair up to the table and spreading out in front of him the various papers upon which were recorded the antics of the dancing men. "As to you, friend Watson, I owe you every atonement for having allowed your natural curiosity to remain so long unsatisfied. To you, inspector, the whole incident may appeal as a remarkable professional study. I must tell you first of all the interesting circumstances connected with the previous consultations which Mr. Hilton Cubitt has had with me in Baker Street." He then shortly recapitulated the facts which have already been recorded. "I have here in front of me these singular productions, at which one might smile had they not proved them- selves to be the fore-runners of so terrible a tragedy. I am fairly familiar with all forms of secret writings, and am myself the author of a trifling monograph upon the subject, in which I analyze one hundred and sixty separate ciphers; but I confess that this is entirely new to me. The object of those who in- vented the system has apparently been to conceal that these characters convey a message, and to give the idea that they are the mere random sketches of children.

"Having once recognised, however, that the symbols stood for letters, and having applied the rules which guide us in all forms of secret writings, the solution was easy enough. The first message submitted to me was so short that it was impossible for me to do more than to say with some confidence that the symbol

stood for E. As you are aware, E is the most common letter in the English alphabet, and it pre- dominates to so marked an extent that even in a short sentence one would expect to find it most often. Out of fifteen symbols in the first message four were the same, so it was reasonable to set this down as E. It is true that in some cases the figure was bearing a flag and in some cases not, but it was probable from the way in which the flags were dis- tributed that they were used to break the sentence up into words. I accepted this as a hypothesis, and noted that E was represented by

"But now came the real difficulty of the inquiry. The order of the English letters after E is by no means well marked, and any preponderance which may be shown in an average of a printed sheet may be reversed in a single short sentence. Speaking roughly, T, A, O, I, N, S, H, R, D, and L are the numerical order in which letters occur; but T, A, O, and I are very nearly abreast of each other, and it would be an endless task to try each combination until a meaning was arrived at. I, therefore, waited for fresh material. In my second interview with Mr. Hilton Cubitt he was able to give me two other short sentences and one message, which appeared—since there was no flag—to be a single word. Here are the symbols. Now, in the single word I have already got the two E's coming second and fourth in a word of five letters. It might be 'sever,' or 'lever,' or 'never.' There can be no question that the latter as a reply to an

appeal is far the most probable, and the circumstances pointed to its being a reply written by the lady.
Accepting it as correct, we are now able to say that the symbols

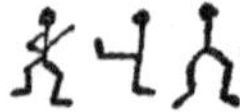

stand respectively for N, V, and R.

"Even now I was in considerable difficulty, but a happy thought put me in possession of several other letters. It occurred to me that if these appeals came, as I expected, from someone who had been intimate with the lady in her early life, a combi- nation which contained two E's with three letters between might very well stand for the name 'ELSIE.' On examination I found that such a combination formed the termination of the message which was three times repeated. It was certainly some appeal to 'Elsie.' In this way I had got my L, S, and I. But what appeal could it be? There were only four letters in the word which preceded 'Elsie,' and it ended in E. Surely the word must be 'COME.' I tried all other four letters ending in E, but could find none to fit the case. So now I was in possession of C, O, and M, and I was in a position to attack the first message once more, dividing it into words and putting dots for each symbol which was still unknown. So treated it worked out in this fashion:

.M .ERE ..E SL.NE.

"Now the first letter can only be A, which is a most useful discovery, since it occurs no fewer than three

times in this short sentence, and the H is also ap-
parent in the second word. Now it becomes:

AM HERE A.E SLANE.

Or, filling in the obvious vacancies in the name: AM
HERE ABE SLANEY.

I had so many letters now that I could proceed with
considerable confidence to the second message, which
worked out in this fashion:

A. ELRI.ES.

Here I could only make sense by putting T and G for the
missing letters, and supposing that the name was that
of some house or inn at which the writer was staying.”

Inspector Martin and I had listened with the utmost
interest to the full and clear account of how my friend
had produced results which had led to so complete a
command over our difficulties.

“What did you do then, sir?” asked the inspector.

“I had every reason to suppose that this Abe Slaney was
an American, since Abe is an American contraction,
and since a letter from America had been the starting-
point of all the trouble. I had also every cause to think
that there was some criminal secret in the matter. The
lady’s allusions to her past and her refusal to take her
husband into her confidence both pointed in that
direction. I therefore cabled to my friend, Wilson
Hargreave, of the New York Police Bureau, who has
more than once made use of my knowledge of London

crime. I asked him whether the name of Abe Slaney was known to him. Here is his reply: 'The most dangerous crook in Chicago.' On the very evening upon which I had his answer Hilton Cubitt sent me the last message from Slaney. Working with known letters it took this form:

ELSIE .RE.ARE TO MEET THY GO.

The addition of a P and a D completed a message which showed me that the rascal was proceeding from persuasion to threats, and my knowledge of the crooks of Chicago prepared me to find that he might very rapidly put his words into action. I at once came to Norfolk with my friend and colleague, Dr. Watson, but, unhappily, only in time to find that the worst had already occurred."

"It is a privilege to be associated with you in the handling of a case," said the inspector, warmly. "You will excuse me, however, if I speak frankly to you. You are only answerable to yourself, but I have to answer to my superiors. If this Abe Slaney, living at Elrige's, is indeed the murderer, and if he has made his escape while I am seated here, I should certainly get into serious trouble."

"You need not be uneasy. He will not try to escape."

"How do you know?"

"To fly would be a confession of guilt." "Then let us go to arrest him."

"I expect him here every instant." "But why should he come?"

"Because I have written and asked him."

"But this is incredible, Mr. Holmes! Why should he come because you have asked him? Would not such a request rather rouse his suspicions and cause him to fly?"

"I think I have known how to frame the letter," said Sherlock Holmes. "In fact, if I am not very much mistaken, here is the gentleman himself coming up the drive."

A man was striding up the path which led to the door. He was a tall, handsome, swarthy fellow, clad in a suit of grey flannel, with a Panama hat, a bristling black beard, and a great, aggressive hooked nose, and flourishing a cane as he walked. He swaggered up the path as if the place belonged to him, and we heard his loud, confident peal at the bell.

"I think, gentlemen," said Holmes, quietly, "that we had best take up our position behind the door. Every precaution is necessary when dealing with such a fellow. You will need your handcuffs, inspector. You can leave the talking to me."

We waited in silence for a minute—one of those minutes which one can never forget. Then the door opened and the man stepped in. In an instant Holmes clapped a pistol to his head and Martin slipped the handcuffs over his wrists. It was all done so swiftly and deftly that the fellow was help- less before he knew that he was attacked. He glared from one to the other of us with a pair of blazing black eyes. Then he burst into a bitter laugh.

"Well, gentlemen, you have the drop on me this time. I seem to have knocked up against something hard. But I came here in answer to a letter from Mrs. Hilton Cubitt. Don't tell me that she is in this? Don't tell me that she helped to set a trap for me?"

"Mrs. Hilton Cubitt was seriously injured and is at death's door."

The man gave a hoarse cry of grief which rang through the house.

"You're crazy!" he cried, fiercely. "It was he that was hurt, not she. Who would have hurt little Elsie? I may have threatened her, God forgive me, but I would not have touched a hair of her pretty head. Take it back— you! Say that she is not hurt!"

"She was found badly wounded by the side of her dead husband."

He sank with a deep groan on to the settee and buried his face in his manacled hands. For five minutes he was silent. Then he raised his face once more, and spoke with the cold composure of despair.

"I have nothing to hide from you, gentlemen," said he. "If I shot the man he had his shot at me, and there's no murder in that. But if you think I could have hurt that woman, then you don't know either me or her. I tell you there was never a man in this world loved a woman more than I loved her. I had a right to her. She was pledged to me years ago. Who was this Englishman that he should come between us? I tell you that I had the first right to her, and that I was only claiming my own."

"She broke away from your influence when she found the man that you are," said Holmes, sternly. "She fled from America to avoid you, and she married an honourable gentleman in England. You dogged her and followed her and made her life a misery to her in order to induce her to abandon the husband whom she loved and respected in order to fly with you, whom she feared and hated. You have ended by bringing about the death of a noble man and driving his wife to suicide. That is your record in this business, Mr. Abe Slaney, and you will answer for it to the law."

"If Elsie dies I care nothing what becomes of me," said the American. He opened one of his hands and looked at a note crumpled up in his palm. "See here, mister," he cried, with a gleam of suspicion in his eyes, "you're not trying to scare me over this, are you? If the lady is hurt as bad as you say, who was it that wrote this note?" He tossed it forwards on to the table.

"I wrote it to bring you here."

"You wrote it? There was no one on earth out- side the Joint who knew the secret of the dancing men. How came you to write it?"

"What one man can invent another can dis- cover," said Holmes. "There is a cab coming to convey you to Norwich, Mr. Slaney. But, mean- while, you have time to make some small reparation for the injury you have wrought. Are you aware that Mrs. Hilton Cubitt has herself lain under grave suspicion of the murder of her husband, and that it was only my presence here and the knowledge which I happened to possess which has saved her from the accusation? The least that you owe her is to make it clear to the whole world that she was in no way, directly or indirectly, responsible for his tragic end.”

“I ask nothing better,” said the American. “I guess the very best case I can make for myself is the absolute naked truth.”

“It is my duty to warn you that it will be used against you,” cried the inspector, with the magnificent fair-play of the British criminal law.

Slaney shrugged his shoulders.

“I’ll chance that,” said he. “First of all, I want you gentlemen to understand that I have known this lady since she was a child. There were seven of us in a gang in Chicago, and Elsie’s father was the boss of the Joint. He was a clever man, was old Patrick. It was he who invented that writing, which would pass as a child’s scrawl unless you just happened to have the key to it. Well, Elsie learned some of our ways; but she couldn’t stand the business, and she had a bit of honest money of her own, so she gave us all the slip and got away to London. She had been engaged to me, and she would have married me, I believe, if I had taken over another profession; but she would have nothing to do with anything on the cross. It was only after her marriage to this Englishman that I was able to find out where she was. I wrote to her, but got no answer. After that I came over, and, as letters were no use, I put my messages where she could read them.

"Well, I have been here a month now. I lived in that farm, where I had a room down below, and could get in and out every night, and no one the wiser. I tried all I could to coax Elsie away. I knew that she read the messages, for once she wrote an answer under one of them. Then my temper got the better of me, and I began to threaten her. She sent me a letter then, imploring me to go away and saying that it would break her heart if any scandal should come upon her husband. She said that she would come down when her husband was asleep at three in the morning, and speak with me through the end window, if I would go away afterwards and leave her in peace. She came down and brought money with her, trying to bribe me to go. This made me mad, and I caught her arm and tried to pull her through the window. At that moment in rushed the husband with his revolver in his hand. Elsie had sunk down upon the floor, and we were face to face. I was heeled also, and I held up my gun to scare him off and let me get away. He fired and missed me. I pulled off almost at the same instant, and down he dropped. I made away across the garden, and as I went I heard the window shut behind me. That's God's truth, gentlemen, every word of it, and I heard no more about it until that lad came riding up with a note which made me walk in here, like a jay, and give myself into your hands."

A cab had driven up whilst the American had been talking. Two uniformed policemen sat inside. Inspector Martin rose and touched his prisoner on the shoulder.

"It is time for us to go." "Can I see her first?"

"No, she is not conscious. Mr. Sherlock Holmes, I only hope that if ever again I have an important case I shall have the good fortune to have you by my side."

We stood at the window and watched the cab drive away. As I turned back my eye caught the pellet of paper which the prisoner had tossed upon the table. It was the note with which Holmes had decoyed him.

"See if you can read it, Watson," said he, with a smile.

It contained no word, but this little line of dancing men:

"If you use the code which I have explained," said Holmes, "you will find that it simply means 'Come here at once.' I was convinced that it was an invitation which he would not refuse, since he could never imagine that it could come from any- one but the lady. And so, my dear Watson, we have ended by turning the dancing men to good when they have so often been the agents of evil, and I think that I have fulfilled my promise of giving you something unusual for your note-book. Three-forty is our train, and I fancy we should be back in Baker Street for dinner."

Only one word of epilogue. The American, Abe Slaney, was condemned to death at the winter as- sizes at Norwich; but his penalty was changed to penal servitude in consideration of mitigating circumstances, and the certainty that Hilton Cubitt had fired the first shot. Of Mrs. Hilton Cubitt I only know that I have heard she recovered entirely, and that she still remains a widow, devoting her whole life to the care of the poor and to the administration of her husband's estate.

List of Refences

20th Century Fox ; Dreamworks Animation ; directed by Chris Sanders & Kirk DeMicco ; produced by Kristine Belson, Jane Hartwell ; screenplay by Kirk DeMicco & Chris Sanders ; story by John Cleese, Kirk DeMicco, Chris Sanders. (2013). The Croods. Beverly Hills, Calif. :Twentieth Century Fox Home Entertainment

Ali-Karamali, Sumbul (2008). The Muslim Next Door: The Qur'an, the Media, and That Veil Thing. White Cloud Press. pp. 240–241.

Andrews, M., Chapman, B., & Purcell, S. (2012). Brave. Walt Disney Studios Motion Pictures.

Ash Brannon, C. B., Mychael Danna, Nicholas Dodd, Liza Richardson, D. P. & Nicholas Dodd, M. D. (2007) SURF'S UP. USA.

Bancroft, T., & Cook, B. (1998). Mulan. Buena Vista Pictures.

Bird, B., & Pinkava, J. (2007). Ratatouille. Buena Vista Pictures.

Bruchac, J. (2006). Code talker: a novel about the Navajo Marines of World War Two. [Literature circle ed.]. New York, Scholastic, Inc.

Doyle, Arthur Conan, 1859-1930. The Complete Sherlock Holmes. Garden City, N.Y. :Doubleday & Co., 1930.

https://allpoetry.com/poem/8543567-Opportunity-by-Edward-Rowland-Sill

https://www.bevdoolittle.net/

https://www.smithsonianmag.com/smart-news/sherlock-holmes-now-officially-copyright-and-open-business-180951794/

Osborne, M., & Stevenson, J. (2008). Kung Fu Panda. Paramount Pictures.

Penny, L., & Cosham, R. (2016). The Brutal Telling. Unabridged. [United States], Macmillan Audio.

Shadyac, T. (1998). Patch Adams. Universal Pictures.

Stanton, A., Unkrich, L., Peterson, B., Reynolds, D., Brooks, A., DeGeneres, E., Gould, A., & Newman, T. (2003). Finding Nemo. Collector's ed., widescreen and fullscreen. Burbank, CA, Distributed by Buena Vista Home Entertainment.

Stirling, S. M. (2006). The protector's war: a novel of the change. New York, ROC, an imprint of New American Library.

Turteltaub, J. (Director). (1996). Phenomenon [Film]. Touchstone Pictures.

Tzu, S. (2010). *The art of war*. Capstone Publishing.

Wikipedia contributors. (2024, May 23). Caesar cipher. In *Wikipedia, The Free Encyclopedia*. Retrieved 19:02, May 31, 2024, from https://en.wikipedia.org/w/index.php?title=Caesar_cipher&oldid=1225214144

Wikipedia contributors. (2024, May 29). Morse code. In *Wikipedia, The Free Encyclopedia*. Retrieved 22:31, May 31, 2024, from https://en.wikipedia.org/w/index.php?title=Morse_code&oldid=1226202536

R-Jay Wilde lives in Oregon with his remarkably creative, beautiful, super smart wife and their four crazy wild kids. He likes to read, eat lunch, draw, make stuff, play with words and generally breath in and out every day.

Your feedback is appreciated!

Thank you for reading this book!

It's through your feedback, support and reviews that I'm able to create the best books possible.

Please take 60 seconds to leave an honest review of the book and share your feedback and thoughts for others to see.

To do so, find the book on Amazon's website (or wherever you bought the book) and locate the section to leave a review. Select a star rating and write a couple of sentences.

Thank you so much for your support.

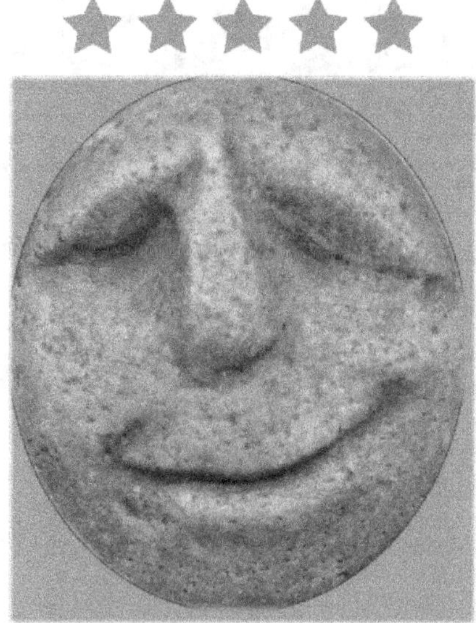

Brought to you by HappyRocks Books.

See all our books at www.rjaywilde.com

Dancing Men Cypher on One Page

a	
b	
c	
d	
e	
f	
g	
h	
i	
j	
k	
l	
m	

n	
o	
p	
q	
r	
s	
t	
u	
v	
w	
x	
y	
z	

0	
1	
2	
3	
4	
5	
6	
7	
8	
9	
!	
@	
$